SLITHERING SNAKES
Anacondas
by Suzane Nguyen
BLASTOFF! READERS 2
BELLWETHER MEDIA • MINNEAPOLIS, MN

Blastoff! Readers are carefully developed by literacy experts to build reading stamina and move students toward fluency by combining standards-based content with developmentally appropriate text.

LEVELS

Level 1 provides the most support through repetition of high-frequency words, light text, predictable sentence patterns, and strong visual support.

Level 2 offers early readers a bit more challenge through varied sentences, increased text load, and text-supportive special features.

Level 3 advances early-fluent readers toward fluency through increased text load, less reliance on photos, advancing concepts, longer sentences, and more complex special features.

★ **Blastoff! Universe**

Reading Level

Grades
1–3

Grade
4

This edition first published in 2025 by Bellwether Media, Inc.

Library of Congress Cataloging-in-Publication Data

Names: Nguyen, Suzane, author.
Title: Anacondas / by Suzane Nguyen.
Description: Minneapolis, MN : Bellwether Media, Inc., 2025. | Series: Blastoff! readers: slithering snakes | Includes bibliographical references and index. | Audience: Ages 5-8 | Audience: Grades K-1 | Summary: "Simple text and full-color photography introduce beginning readers to anacondas. Developed by literacy experts for students in kindergarten through third grade"-- Provided by publisher.
Identifiers: LCCN 2024003111 (print) | LCCN 2024003112 (ebook) | ISBN 9798886870343 (library binding) | ISBN 9781644878781 (ebook)
Subjects: LCSH: Anaconda--Juvenile literature.
Classification: LCC QL666.O63 N48 2025 (print) | LCC QL666.O63 (ebook) | DDC 597.96/7--dc23/eng/20240208
LC record available at https://lccn.loc.gov/2024003111
LC ebook record available at https://lccn.loc.gov/2024003112

Editor: Betsy Rathburn Designer: Brittany McIntosh

Printed in the United States of America, North Mankato, MN.

Table of Contents

Heavyweight Reptiles

Anacondas are the heaviest snakes in the world! There are four types. Green anacondas are the heaviest.

All anacondas live in South America.

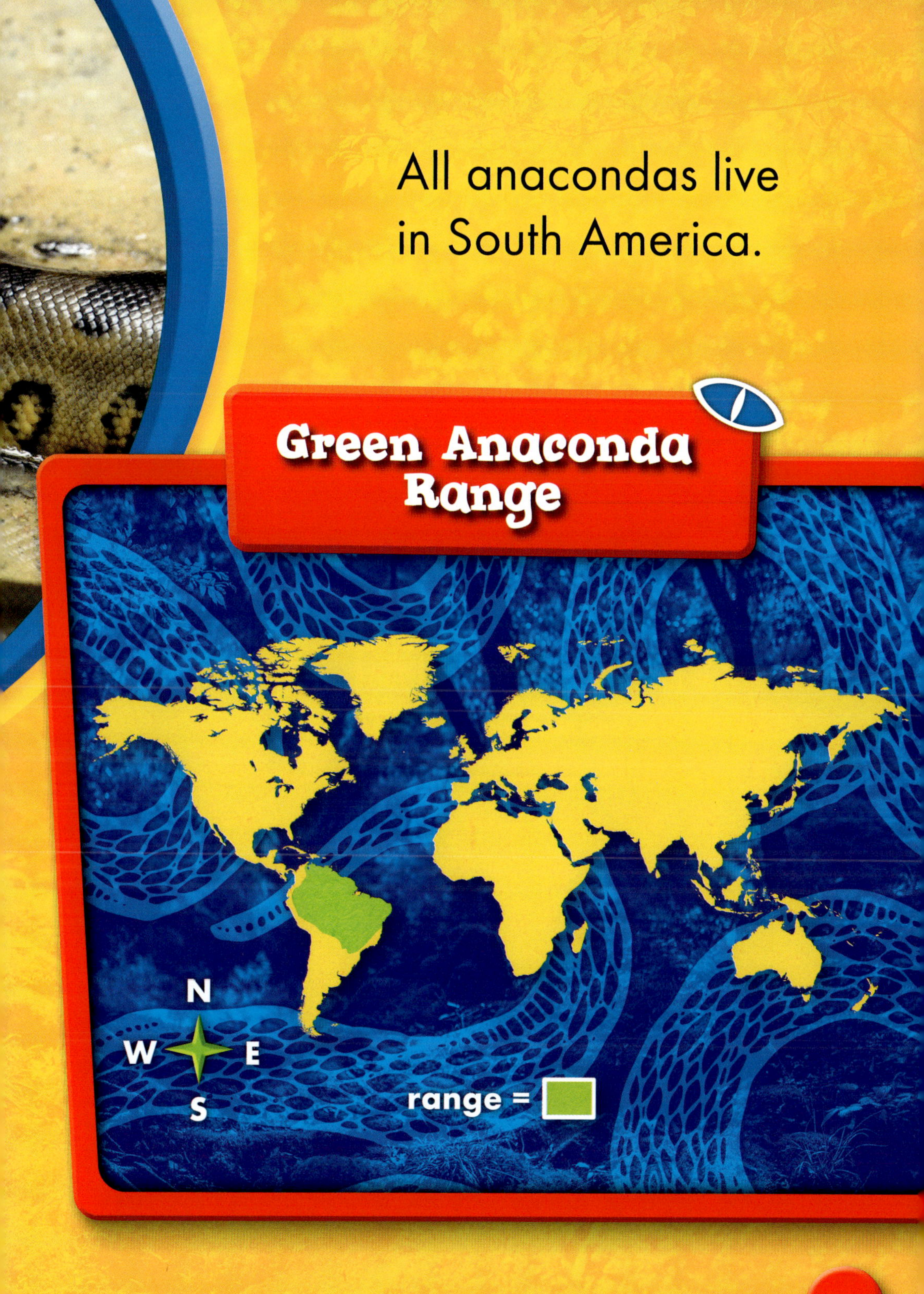

Anacondas grow up to 30 feet (9 meters) long. They weigh up to 550 pounds (249 kilograms)!

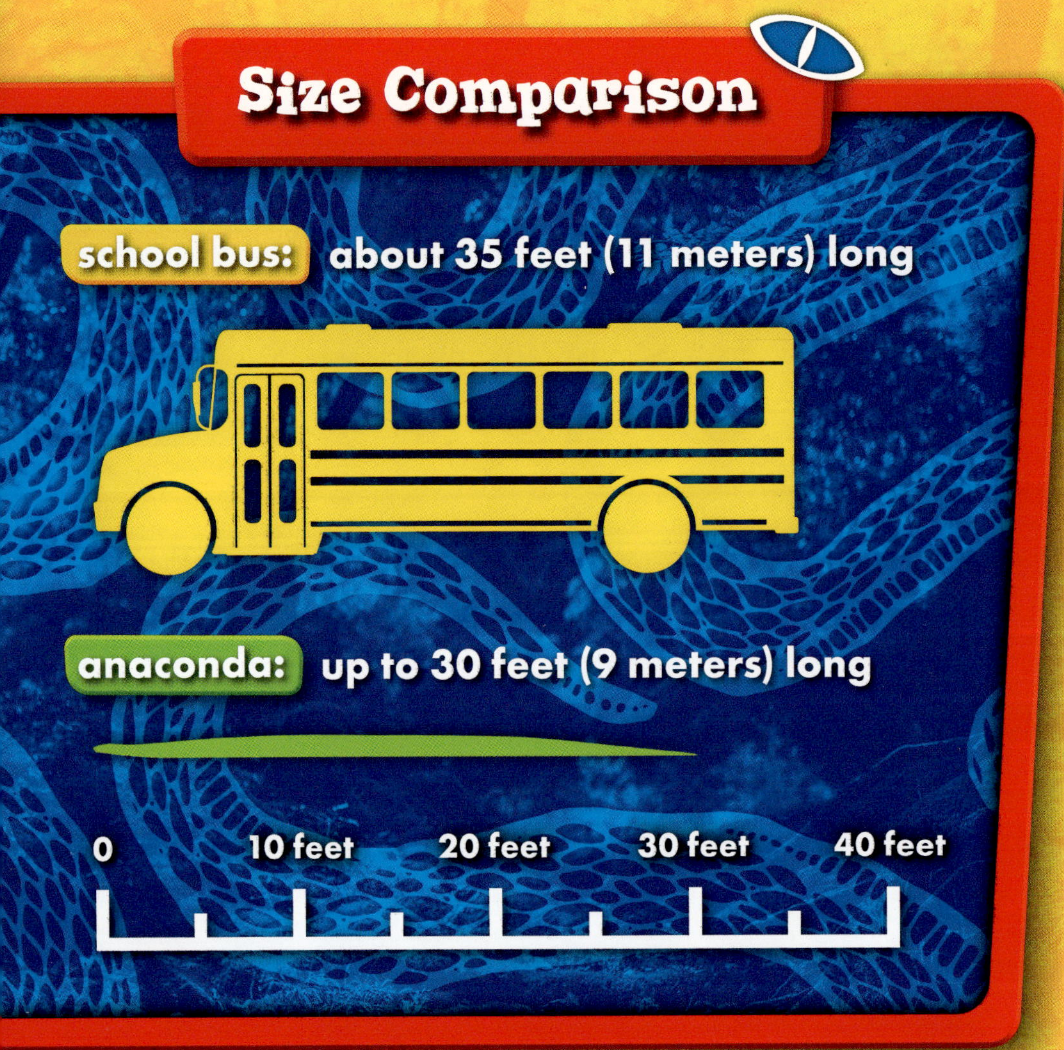

dark-spotted anaconda

Their **scales** are green, brown, or yellow. They may have dark spots.

Their eyes and **nostrils** are on top of their head. This helps them find **prey** underwater.

Long, pointed teeth help them catch meals.

Spot an Anaconda!

Sneaky Hunters

These **reptiles** are
great swimmers.
They mostly live in water.

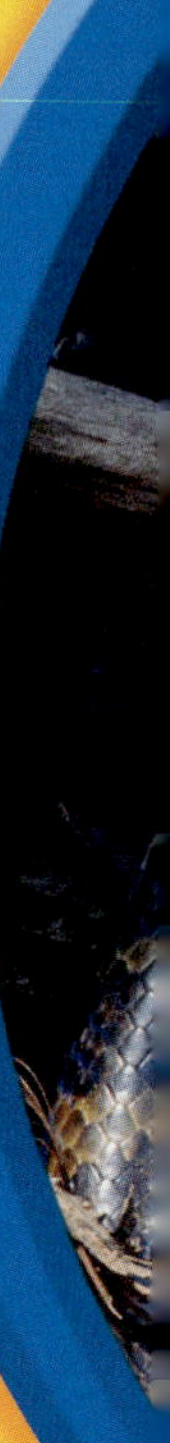

They swim through **swamps** and **rain forests**. They also live in **grasslands**.

Anacondas mostly live alone. They sometimes travel with the seasons.

Their jaws stretch
to open wide. They can
eat prey whole!

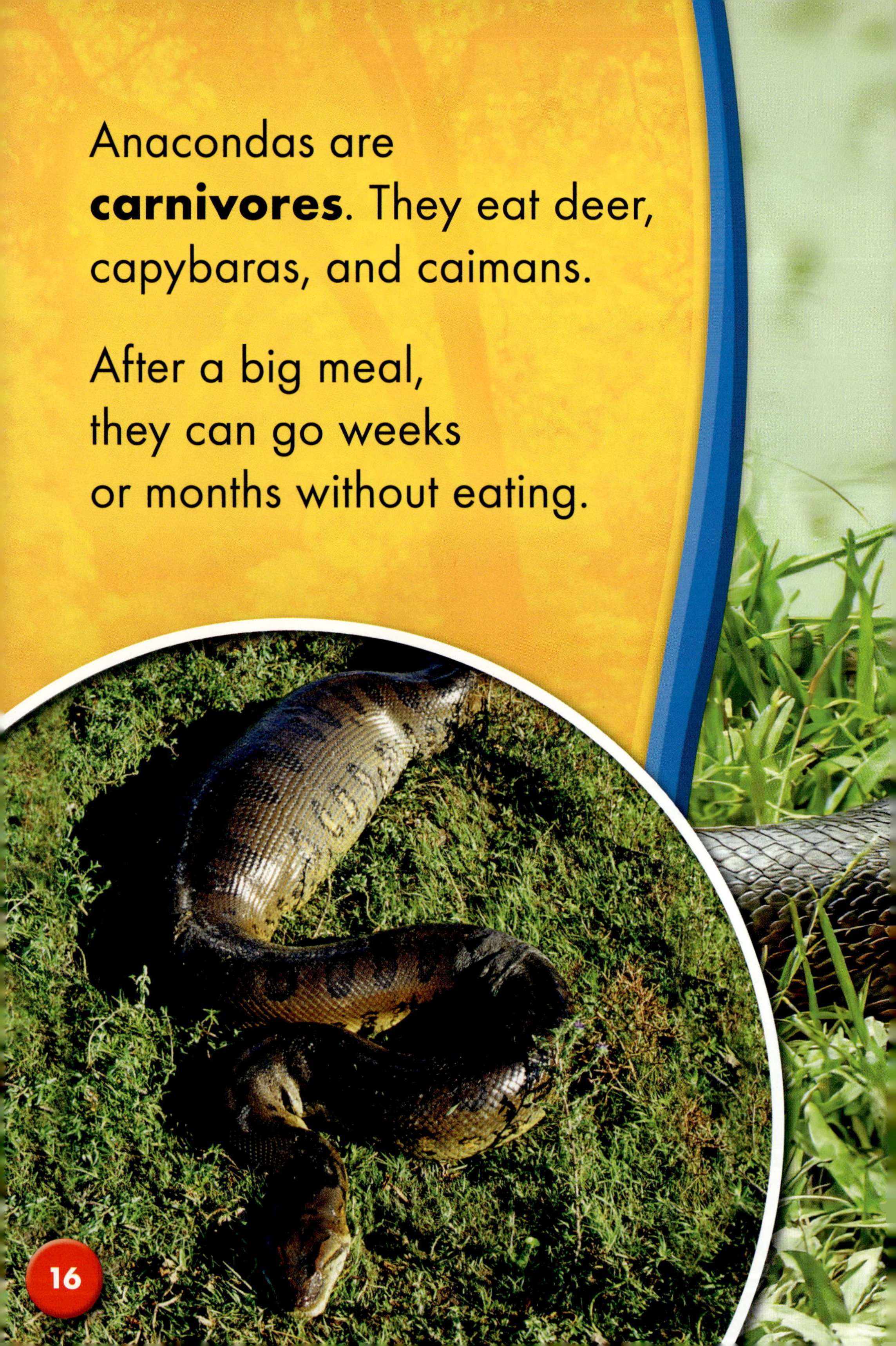

Anacondas are **carnivores**. They eat deer, capybaras, and caimans.

After a big meal, they can go weeks or months without eating.

Anaconda Food
deer
capybaras
caimans

Female anacondas have live young. The snakes usually have 20 to 40 babies at once.

Females have babies every one or two years.

Baby anacondas can swim and hunt right away. They are grown up by around four years old.

The snakes are ready to have young of their own!

Green Anaconda Stats

status in the wild: least concern

life span: up to 10 years

Glossary

carnivores–animals that only eat meat

grasslands–lands covered with grasses and other soft plants with few bushes or trees

nostrils–the two openings of the nose

predators–animals that hunt other animals for food

prey–animals that are hunted by other animals for food

rain forests–thick, green forests that receive a lot of rain

reptiles–cold-blooded animals that have backbones

scales–plates that cover an animal's body

swamps–wetlands filled with trees and other woody plants

threatened–in danger

To Learn More

AT THE LIBRARY

Fenmore, Taylor. *Anacondas: Nature's Biggest Snake.* Minneapolis, Minn.: Lerner Publications, 2024.

Nguyen, Suzane. *Boa Constrictors.* Minneapolis, Minn.: Bellwether Media, 2025.

Thielges, Alissa. *Anacondas.* Mankato, Minn.: Amicus, 2024.

ON THE WEB

FACTSURFER

Factsurfer.com gives you a safe, fun way to find more information.

1. Go to www.factsurfer.com.
2. Enter "anacondas" into the search box and click 🔍.
3. Select your book cover to see a list of related content.

Index

The images in this book are reproduced through the courtesy of: Patrick K. Campbell, front cover, p. 4; cellistka, p. 3; Nature Picture Library/ Alamy, pp. 7, 11; C-images/ Alamy, p. 8; chrisbrignell, p. 9; WaterFrame/ Alamy, p. 10; Karel Bartik, p. 12; Arterra Picture Library/ Alamy, p. 13; SuperStock/ Francois Gohier/ Mary Evans Picture Library, pp. 14, 16; chamleunejai, p. 15; ms_pics_and_more, pp. 16-17; Tom Reichner, p. 17 (deer); Giedriius, p. 17 (capybara); Vaclav Sebek, p. 17 (caiman); simonkr, p. 18; Animals and pictures/ Alamy, p. 19; Uwe Bergwitz, p. 20; SuperStock/ Minden Pictures, pp. 20-21; Nynke van Holten, p. 23.